S0-ARK-574

CHECKERBOARD NATURE LIBRARY

INSECTS

Fireflies

by Cari Meister

GREENWOOD PUBLIC LIBRARY
310 S. MERIDIAN
GREENWOOD, IN 46143

ABDO
Publishing Company

visit us at
www.abdopub.com

Published by ABDO Publishing Company, 4940 Viking Drive, Suite 622, Edina, Minnesota 55435. Copyright © 2001 Abdo Consulting Group, Inc., Pentagon Tower, P.O. Box 36036, Minneapolis, Minnesota 55435 USA. International copyrights reserved in all countries. No part of this book may be reproduced in any form without written permission from the publisher.

Printed in the United States

Illustrators: Edwin Beylerian, Carey Molter

Cover photo: PhotoDisc

Interior photos: Animals Animals, Artville, Corel, Corbis Images, Peter Arnold, Inc., PhotoDisc, PictureQuest

Editors: Tamara L. Britton, Kate A. Furlong

Design and production: MacLean & Tuminelly

Library of Congress Cataloging-in-Publication Data

Meister, Cari.
  Fireflies / Cari Meister.
    p. cm. -- (Insects)
  ISBN 1-57765-462-5
    1. Fireflies--Juvenile literature. [1. Fireflies.] I. Title.

QL596.L28 M45 2000
595.76'44--dc21

00-056882

Contents

What is a Firefly?

Fireflies are like little torches in the night sky. They seem to be sending out secret codes with their flashing lights. In a way, they are.

There are about 2,000 different kinds of fireflies. Each kind of firefly has a special flash code. Fireflies flash this special code to find mates of the same kind.

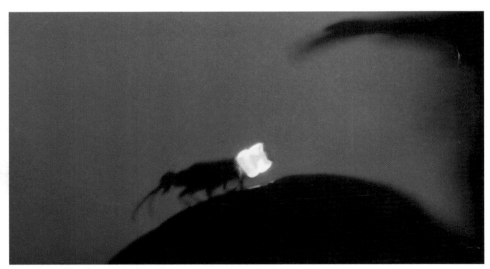

Fireflies flash special codes to attract mates.

Fireflies are not really flies. They are beetles. Most fireflies are less than an inch long. Female fireflies are larger than males. Fireflies are black or brown with orange or red markings.

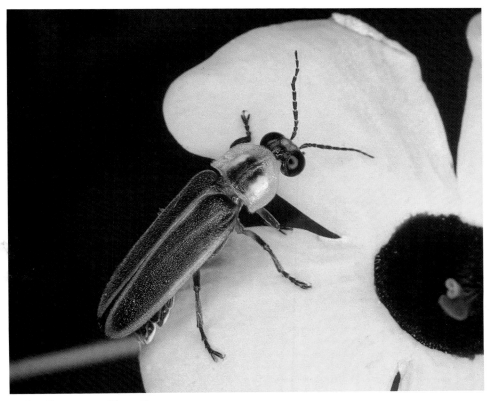

A firefly on a yellow flower.

The Firefly's Body

Fireflies have three main body sections: a head, a thorax, and an abdomen. The first section is the head. The middle part is the thorax. The last part is the abdomen.

head

thorax

leg

abdomen

On the firefly's head are antennae and eyes. Fireflies smell and hear with their antennae. Their big eyes can see in many directions at once.

The firefly's six legs and two sets of wings are on its thorax. The outer wings are hard. They are called elytra. The elytra protect the inner wings that are used for flying. If you looked inside a firefly's thorax, you would see many muscles. The muscles are attached to the wings. Muscles give a firefly power to fly.

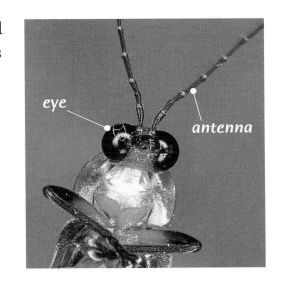

eye

antenna

outer wing (elytra)

inner wing

In the abdomen, Fireflies have special organs called
lanterns. The lantern is what produces the firefly's light.
Fireflies can glow because they have special chemicals inside
their bodies. The chemicals are called luciferase and
luciferin. These chemicals mix with oxygen in the air. When
they mix, a firefly glows. The abdomen also contains the
organs for digestion and mating.

lantern

Fireflies do not have bones, like people. They have **exoskeletons**. The exoskeleton protects the insect's soft inner organs. All of the firefly's muscles are attached to it, too.

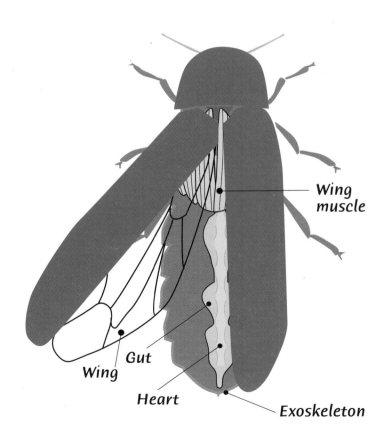

Wing muscle

Gut

Wing

Heart

Exoskeleton

How They Grow

Fireflies go through four growth stages: egg, larva, pupa, and adult. During mating season, male fireflies fly around in the night sky. They flash their lanterns on and off with their own special flash code.

Female fireflies that are ready to mate wait on plant leaves and stems. When a female sees a male flash her special flash code, she flashes it back. Then, the male lands on the plant next to the female and they mate. About five days after mating, the female lays about 500 eggs in a damp place, usually near water.

The eggs hatch into larvae in about a month. The larvae do not look like fireflies at all. They look like worms. Since they glow, firefly larvae are called glowworms.

Firefly larvae.

The **larvae** have two main jobs, to eat and grow. When a larva is ready for the next stage of life, it digs a hole and buries itself.

Inside the hole, the larva **molts** and changes into a **pupa** in about 40 days. Then, the pupa rests for about 10 days. Then, the pupa **emerges** from its covering as an adult firefly. After resting a few days, the adult comes out of the hole and begins looking for a mate.

Firefly pupal skin.

Adult fireflies.

What They Eat

Fireflies eat the most when they are in the **larva** stage of growth. The fat stored in their bodies during this time supports the firefly through its **pupa** and adult stages. So, a larva is always hungry. It spends much of its day eating. Its favorite foods are snails, worms, and other small insects.

This firefly larva is eating a slug.

Some larvae wait in **damp** places until prey comes by. Others go in search of food. When a larva finds a meal, it grabs it with its strong jaws.

A **larva** cannot chew a whole snail or worm into tiny pieces. It has to break down its food before it can eat. When a larva catches a snail or worm, it injects the prey with digestive juices. The juices break down the animal's body. Then, the larva drinks the liquid through hollow **mouthparts**.

Snails and worms are two of a firefly larva's favorite foods.

This firefly is drinking plant juice.

Some adult fireflies eat **nectar** from flowers. Some drink dew from leaves. But most do not eat or drink at all.

Where They Live

Fireflies live all over the world. They live on every continent except Antarctica. Firefly **larvae** like **damp**, dark places. They like to hide under big rocks, piles of leaves, or rotting logs. They also like to live underwater in rivers, lakes, or swamps.

Fireflies like to rest on leaves and rotting logs.

14

Adult fireflies spend most of their time in the air. Male fireflies spend more time in the air than female fireflies. Female fireflies spend more time on leaves, waiting to mate.

When the adult fireflies are not mating, they live in trees or bushes. Most fireflies are nocturnal. This means that they rest at home during the day and go out at night.

Most fireflies are active at night.

GREENWOOD PUBLIC LIBRARY
310 S. MERIDIAN
GREENWOOD, IN 46143

Enemies

Fireflies have many enemies. Birds, frogs, fish, and toads like to eat firefly **larvae**. Large beetles also like to eat the larvae. The larvae try to hide from their enemies. They hide under rocks, sticks, and leaves. Even when they are eating, they try to find cover.

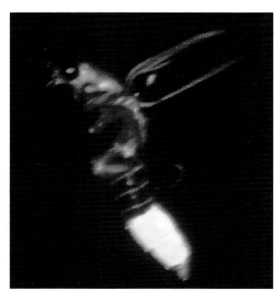

Fireflies hunt at night to avoid enemies.

Firefly larvae hunt at night. That way, it is harder for **predators** to see them. Some kinds of firefly larvae are poisonous. They squirt the poison from their bodies when a predator tries to eat them.

When young fireflies grow up, they have new enemies. A spider is an adult firefly's worst enemy. Fireflies get caught in spider webs. Unable to get free, they become the spider's meal.

A spider is an adult firefly's worst enemy.

Beetles and frogs eat firefly larvae.

Fireflies & People

Fireflies are not harmful to people. In fact, they can be useful. In some parts of the world, fireflies are used as flashlights. In South America, some people put fireflies in net bags. They attach the bags to their ankles and wrists. This way, when they are traveling at night, they can see. The fireflies light the way.

In Japan, people make firefly lanterns. The lanterns light up night parties. Some outdoor restaurants in Asia use firefly lanterns instead of candles.

Lanterns like this one are made to hold fireflies.

18

Fireflies have even been used in hospitals. One time in Cuba, the lights in a hospital went out. The doctor was in the middle of an operation. He used a firefly lantern to finish it.

Today, doctors are using luciferin and luciferase to help find damaged cells in people.

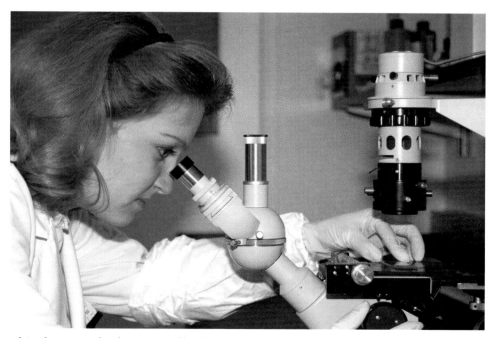

This doctor is looking at cells through a microscope.

Fun Facts

🐝 The firefly is Pennsylvania's state insect.

🐝 A firefly's glow is not hot. It is a cold light.

🐝 Not all kinds of fireflies can glow.

🐝 Fireflies glow brighter in warm weather than in cold weather. The temperature also effects the speed of the flashing.

🐝 The female Photuris firefly is **carnivorous**. She tricks male fireflies to come to her by imitating their special flashing code. When they fly over and land on her leaf, she eats them.

A female photuris firefly eats a male firefly.

To make a firefly **lantern**, poke holes in the top of a jar so that the fireflies can breathe. Catch fireflies and put them in the jar. Put a wet paper towel in the jar with them. Make sure to let your fireflies go at the end of the night.

Here is an illustration of a firefly lantern.

Glossary

carnivorous – meat-eating.

damp – slightly wet.

emerge – to come out.

exoskeleton – the outer casing that protects an insect.

lantern – the organ on a firefly where light is made. Also, a portable light.

larva – the second stage in the life of a firefly. Larvae means more than one larva.

molt – to shed old skin and replace it with a new skin.

mouthparts – a structure near the mouth that an insect uses to eat.

nectar – a sweet liquid produced by some flowers.

predator – an animal that kills and eats other animals.

pupa – the third stage in the life of a firefly, when the larva is changing into an adult firefly.

Web Sites

http://www.ent.iastate.edu/misc/insectsasfood.html
    Insect Recipes
    This site hosted by Iowa State University has several
    tasty insect recipes with nutrition facts and sources for
    buying the bugs.

http://everest.ento.vt.edu/~carroll/insect_video_home.html
    Insects in Motion
    This site from Virginia Tech has short films of different
    insect behavior. The clips are in Quicktime movie
    format.

http://www.ex.ac.uk/bugclub/
    Join The Bug Club
    This site for young entomologists includes a newsletter,
    puzzles, and games.

*These sites are subject to change. Go to your favorite search engine
and type in Fireflies for more sites.*

Index